"Sometimes I feel sorry for hetero writers! So much of their relationships is prescribed and the challenge is up to the artist to present relationships in a new way without destroying expectations. I'm happy to say Rich Murphy ignores all these directives as nonsense. His poems are maps of complicated straight lovers; the keys to this book are the strict use of language and love of discovery."
—Rane Arroyo, author of *The Buried Sea: New and Selected Poems*

"In Rich Murphy's outlandish fables we recognize our lives. The secret is out—'Cupid's Hell Game' has led Romeo and Juliet into the dark caves of modern domesticity. He takes us through those slippery caves with a syntax of entanglement that maps erotic traps and arcs of error. His sinewy language presses against the heavy 'lode' of disillusionment. Detached but far from dispassionate, he watches Adam and Eve tie knots around each other, then he makes of this marriage mess an unforgettable lyric dance."
—Bonnie Costello, author of *Planets on Tables: Poetry, Still Life and the Turning World*

"Unabashed and unsentimental, *Voyeur* discloses an honest pursuit of desire's glorious blunders at the edges of lust, compassion, and love. Murphy's patient, apt concern with poetic form, compressed imagery, and layered metaphor engenders this brisk gathering of two-dozen reality-tales of 'Bunglers / and Klutzes [who] carry headstones for their hearts.' From the grist of quotidian events and observations, Murphy rescues accidental beauty. These poems stride with trenchant whimsy."
—W. Scott Howard, poet and editor of *Reconfigurations: A Journal of Poetics & Poetry / Literature and Culture*

"In *Voyeur*, Rich Murphy earnestly explores the complicated nature and innate integrity of the 'wild' -or even divine - feminine as subject to chance, circumstance, and interaction with the masculine. In some sense, a pervasive longing at once subtle and tense, for a 'natural life,' defines this collection of poems. Murphy's *Voyeur*, while never revealing the *I*, bares a sensitive and often perplexed masculine narrator. But this bemusement, and a masculine struggle to fathom the feminine, is essential to the manuscript; it is the elemental brightening force of this aptly titled collection – a vision to previously veiled poetic spaces. While Murphy's poems are most often set in a contemporary world of suburban gyms and

kitchen tables, they nonetheless draw from aspects of Greek mythology, recalling the Homeric king Odysseus and sorceress Circe; however, as in the centuries-old tract established by the poet Sappho, Murphy's paramount focus rests not on stories of gods and heroes but rather in the quiet sublime of the turning of hours in a life at once familiar and heterodox."
—Ginger Knowlton, poet and artist

"In Rich Murphy's exciting and sexy collection *Voyeur* 'men / and women fall in love with their minor / economies and haggle over appearances /and favors.' Murphy reveals to us that 'I pan from coast to coast / and bedrooms frame acts of the American / Dream in abandon.' Like family, *Voyeur* is complex yet accessible, and Murphy's powerful use of metaphor will intrigue you, 'Husbands and wives fill houses/ with doodads and two strangers.' But also 'father's fetishes, mother's moods, / and aunt's angst, are wrapped in love.' *Voyeur* is a reflection of the family seen through the eyes of an extremely gifted poet."
—Leah Maines, author of *Beyond the River* and *Looking to the East with Western Eyes*

"If Rich Murphy's poems don't get under your skin, if you're not itching to read and reread them, you're not paying attention: 'epiphanies like rashes along your /backbone, and up your legs, and around your scalp as though you were a citizen / on several planets in the universe.' If Trakl, or Kafka, or Wittgenstein, could Twitter the US of the 21st century, would we stumble on language like this: 'Astronomy's gibberish -**+x8#? / while biochemistry !:!:!'? Thinking and feeling on a single plane, in the multi-galactic, Discursive Drift, isn't an option; on Plantagenet Murphy, every distych and DipStych is under construction. That conceit we thought poetry wanted- 'The adhesive ligaments of metaphor'-might become a black hole? Bring your Hummers and commas and Kleats."
— Jonathan Monroe, author of *Demosthenes' Legacy*

"Poetry editors learn quickly to perk up when opening submissions from certain authors. So it is when Rich Murphy shows up in my inbox. Poets who struggle with line limits—and all writers who struggle with word-count limits--can learn much from Rich's shortest poems of, oh, *five words*. I mean, we're getting into *Jesus wept* territory, here. Rich's poems, like bullets, are small things capable of considerable impact."
—Dale Wisely, poet and editor of *Right Hand Pointing*

Voyeur

Rich Murphy

Arlington, Virginia

Published by Gival Press, an imprint of Gival Press, LLC.
For information please write:
Gival Press, LLC, P. O. Box 3812, Arlington, VA 22203.
Website: *www.givalpress.com*

First edition ISBN: 978.1.928589.48.8
Library of Congress Control Number: 2009932063

Bookcover artwork "Bed" © 2009 by Mark Johnson; photo by Matt Murphy.
Photo of Rich Murphy by Bonnie Martin.
Format and design by Ken Schellenberg.

Acknowledgments

The following poems appeared in a chapbook titled *Family Secret* published by Finishing Line Press: The Ark of Oops, Lode Lore, Skating Lessons, Folk Art, Bonanza, Wow Vow, Ravishing, Mass Consumption, Chemical Waste, Valentine Party, Pathos Eros, Love Story, Biological Distraction, Petty Thieves, Family Business, The Guise, Coat-Tail, Living, Downtown, Lullaby, Chaeronea's Conquerors, X-Rated, Casanova's Bossa Nova, Don Juan in America, Romeo's Ruse.

The Ark of Oops, Coat-Tail Living, The Guise, Ravishing, Love Story, and Family Business in *Starry Night Review*

A Wag in Borderlands: Texas Poetry Review

Lode Lore in Blue Fifth Review

From Swoon to Croon and Wow Vow in *Grasslands Review*

Skating Lessons in Emily Dickinson Anthology

Frigid Air, Flora, Accessories, Gretel to Naïve, Her Morning Gargle, and Magic by Design in *Segue Journal*

Spin Cycles and Big Cars, Slut, Pop, and The Woman Wrestler in *Nuvein Magazine*

Pathos Eros in *Ghoti Magazine*

Bonanza in Barrelhouse Review

Mass Consumption and Chemical Waste in *New Delta Review*

The Complements of the House in Words – Myth A Quarterly Poetry Journal

Boxes of Lust and Jingle on the Boardwalk in *Projected Letters*

Natural Disasters, Biological Distraction, Sports Trivia, and Chaeronea's Conquerors in *Inertia Magazine*

Labors of Love in *Whimperbang*

The Guise, Pop, Gretel to Naïve, Her Morning Gargle, and Labors of Love were republished in the Housewife issue of *Cliterature*

Petty Thieves in *essence*

Gender Universes in Cherry Blossom Review

Voyeur and Attention in *Voices*

The Websters et al in *Talking River Review*

No Match in Salamander Magazine

Valentine Party, Blueprint, and Isle of Man in *Red China*

Folk Art in *Foam:e*

Lullaby in Words and Images

Terrorized in Pedestal Magazine

Totalitarian Jig in *Big Toe Review*

Philomela's Reading and Downtown in *Tryst*

X-Rated in Entelechy: Mind and Culture

Boy Meets Girl in *Red Booth*

Casanova's Bossa Nova, Don Juan in America, and Romeo's Ruse in *Poetry*

The Titanic Sea in *Miranda Literary Magazine*

Thanks to Kathleen Spivack who helped me organize the early manuscript.

For Jacqueline, Elizabeth, and Bonnie

"only when women no longer live their lives isolated in
houses and the stories of men."

Carolyn Heilbrun
Writing a Woman's Life

Table of Contents

The Ark of Oops

"So, the word wild here is not used in its modern pejorative sense, meaning out of control, but in its original sense, which means to live a natural life, one in which the *criatura,* creature, has innate integrity and healthy boundaries."

Clarissa Pinkola Estes
Women Who Run With the Wolves

THE ARK OF OOPS

Pairs of people have accidents, catch
fevers, and get married. Later, the illness
cures itself, the injury heals, and there
is either divorce or braces-for-two for life.

Whole lives fly head over heels in domestic slips.
A hermit wonders why people aren't more
careful about falling or why they don't wear
surgical masks when meeting in nightclubs.

No schools have been established to train
teenagers to stay away from high places or tricky
topography or how to wash hands after touching
anyone. People preparing for graduate study believe

that everybody knows from birth how to walk
and breathe with no mistakes, so they study
the sex of all the other animals on earth and play
each night that they are correct. Couples

who put themselves in harm's way for the thrill
of ambulances of physical pleasure understand
nothing from experience ever. The Bunglers
and Klutzes carry headstones for their hearts.

A WAG

My friends act like dogs
and could fill the phone booth
where each calls out to intimacy.
Human beings were sold for parts:

B-movie heroes, soap opera stars,
porn flick sequins. I'm greeted
from the shelters of marriages
that leak isolation on to bones

or from a pack that invites with lines
leashing lingerie to stones.
I'm supposed to sniff the low crotches
of trees and with fashion magazines

chase ministers and priests
before the limousine hits me,
but Superman doesn't use change
to fulfill his flesh with capers

of empathy's live transmigration.
Clerk Kent is a pile of pressed laundry
when I join a seducer's death-march
and am rejected for lack of blindness or fund.

Pst, pants do not exist here,
but hounded by the chill, mismatched
strangers on holiday tear at the moon's
relentless stage direction.

Lode Lore

The mother of lode halved each of her stones
breaking their hearts and scattered them
among time and states. Attracting moons,
compass needles, and refrigerators, the rocks

find it hard to reunite with their genuine fissures
and planes. Tons of dust can blow by before
a magnet stuck in some steel trap recognizes
its Siamese twin was buried in an earthquake

in Bangladesh in the fifteenth century. A Crag
meditates on top of Mount Rainier with high
hopes that an eruption will send it to Zimbabwe
where diamond engagement casts spells

of permanence. Sand compensates around it
expecting to become a river of tiers
sweating the small stuff on the trek down
a living hell to brick and mortar. A real beach

empathizes with the Milky Way's true
unrequited loves but fuses with the nearest cliff
only then to reach out to the cold water reef.
The gravity of a ledge's loneliness from star

to core invites the lure of origin's ore to sculpt
from abandon the energy of artistic masterpieces.

WOM.AN-KIND

A wig, lipstick, and stiletto heels
leaves the biped with two balls
and a bat speechless. The mile
of walking demonstrates empathy

but brings a woman's words no closer.
Lady language, welded and riveted
together by construction crews
enunciating erections that touch

the sky, oozes from petite, cajoled
mouths. An operation's whispering
world, man to vulva, exiles a girl
from the public spheres to "repeat

after me." A pink tot's tongue wields
worlds of foreign tools on its feral
lips over coffee or on a telephone
as though skin were absorbing lotion.

Sentences of intimacy articulate
beneath the weight of frightened
blokes threatened by opinionated
waitresses who with twists of their

wrists serve cocktails. Proficiency
of emotional gesturing hints at
pronunciation of an alphabet too
genetic for even gender benders

whose shoes box sole isolation.

Hormone Olympics

Women and men stand in leotards,
tape, and resin. Barbells litter the gym
floor and dumbbells are set in the bleachers
with the false consciousness of their own
chemistries and genitals. The straight
line, drawn using the shortest distance,
resonates one of two cardboard figures
at its disposal: bow to the monosyllabic
race.
So as not to ruffle feathers
or flop around in jack boots,
most groomed bi-peds press corkscrews
into air or bury them in bottles.
No body lives up to the horizon though.
Muscular kinks and knots,
skeletal mutations, and height restrictions
render gendered imitation steel sujud.
When the other plumbed wannabes
aren't looking, leagues resort
to the fetal position, grip sex
between their many legs
and bend it to each member's wishes.

Labor Law

Men hire women to be children.
Honeymoons continue until babies
fire their bosomless nannies.
The dry nurses to thumb-sucking wives

listen for stirring and a weep, then leap
with diaper and a handyman's tools.
Employees pin paychecks to corsets
and panties, pick up groceries with plastic.

The marriages' C.E.O.s switch hats
to teach family values while their romances
shrink into playpens and breakfast
sausages. The kick and scream

in penthouse command centers
sends forth the subtlest memos
for toys not of men's bodies or minds.
The well-suited infantilizing sitters

employ their weddings to keep
grown ups with hips from stocks
and bonds and from the little boys
who fear the contents of brassieres.

Assembly Required

A first baby step with someone else's equipment
sends pangs from sole to groin.

Neither here nor there,
organs' kleptomaniac, whose mother
outfitted a child with random devices,
jiggles a lever that isn't
and lets a belt cycle for years without question.

Treads of profane loneliness
leave the marks of an armored division
on the speech of the unengendered.

The confusion between social cues and reflexes
reminds absolute strangers of scrambled eggs.
However amazing to rubber stamped folk
though, the owner's feet, unmistakable
to their shoes, choreograph away from the wrestling.

A full-length dressing mirror in public
frightens crowds of stencils.

Bigger strides in the manual
suggest sharing limbs, appendages, and orifices
that do and don't exist.

But the victory of possessing all of oneself
comforts with motion, the only profound love.

FROM SWOON TO CROON

Frank Sinatra was paired with Socrates.
Yeats loved a swan. I was joined to the front half
of a crusader's horse. It was a very good year,
a stranger year though no one realized

anything puzzling about that life. And then
we met our maker. Aristophanes explains
why most of us are such goddamned bastards,
waiting fat and lost for a reunion which would be

of course heaven on Earth. However, the search
seems to lead one to define ownliness, unless
two creative acts crack their performativity
again and again to give birth to lives.

SKATING LESSONS

Two egos' eternal rings
by chance interlocking,
impresses with the prone humps
of eight a bundled Hans,
all hormones below his eyes,
but one, who has observed
the swans, figures out the other world.

Warming my heart over the embers
of extremities at the edge of one
of our millennia, I strap on blades
to slit the throat of winter's white
and survey the planet
for couples falling through ice.

Every single one of us may play hockey
to win an admirer who parallels
our rushes mirroring our broken smiles,
and the species of nations do.

But grace on the frozen lake
of hell to a pair of deaths by drowning,
more life than all family-oriented
suburban neighborhoods, is the embrace
to forge two skates to keep each self at bay.

Frigid Air

Two huskies pulled the bride
over glacial lace and across the tundra grate
deep into the middle of no one. The throbbing
monotony senses ice castles and clowns:
mush, mush, and mush.
The global positioning units rolling
in two facial sockets congratulate the rest.
Before the prick and goose
down, generations of women
and a picture book fluffed
swan feathers and lined a mold
with fresh linen to ready the sledge.
Female breath that steam trunks hold
after the age of ten, fill with costumes
leaving behind a warm outline
that promised a whole. The snowshoes
and roseola nose, forcing a laugh,
coordinate skating on thin mirrors
and actress paint. Dwarfs and hunters
own their own igloos and side-by-side
comforters. Angel powder and puff
applications complete 0, and rescue
another question mark with isolation.

Coat-Tail Living

With a shovel and apologetic smile,
each personal secretary travels through
a life behind a man. Along the highways
and byways, the two-legged horse

fills a suit with matching pockets
for bringing home, while the silent life coach
offers the requisite blushes and scoops
the refuse of the grab and nab. Ever since

shoulder mass won the attention of the public,
breasts and hips pulled up the rear and used
beauty as far as it goes. When the accessory
becomes collaborator, innocence acts

its scene for the audience. Over perks
and benefits the one-person clean-up crew
salivates, and the work horse or thoroughbred
in shoes distributes the bonus of his return.

Spin Cycles and Big Cars

Spouses collaborate against the world,
robbing anyone sleeping alone
and picking the pockets of less-skilled
teams when they can. The desperado duos

blow smoke and hold mirrors hostage
around wallets in each other's homes.
The bystander without a small band
for thuggery is left for dead, a teenager,

honest, after taxes and a holiday season.
Just try to keep the children out of this:
"Bobsey Twins Pin Pets in Their Pens."
When the city malls bless the lonely

or college colleagues into a couple
of crooks and their menace is proclaimed
in hall and haven, the highways are
diverted and sports stadiums catch fire.

Pathos Eros

The tit-for-tat of domestic inmates
courts vacation homes, automobiles,
and golf courses. We sip our due
from each other's shoes

to free our mattress of sides.
Passionate to secure the potential
contents of the other's pockets,
the sex partners executing business feats

with bubbles of imitation celebrity,
skin the knees of their spoiled children
who are groomed, each to share
a slow death with a spiteful stranger.

From among the thieves that marriage
alarms with its vaults and customer service,
two millionaires dance drunk
from behind one another's eyes: one

emulates the palm of a hand; the other
assimilates the teeth of a smile.

BONANZA

Through gold dust, granite, and coal
a man and a woman dig for a diamond.
Entering another dream world of pickaxes
with flashlights strapped to their heads,

they shovel bones out of bed. Deposits of limestone
and lapis lazuli are piled in the bathroom
and kitchen. A Parakeet chirps on the shoulder
of a coat rack, and braces creak during the daily

commute. The miners' veins could detonate
the earth beneath the feet of sexual selection's
reveler picking up stones. Train loads of lode
empty into the mid-life of the mole-eyed couple

scaling shale to exit their oily cave and close
their polar eyes. Queer through the engagement
rings in the back pockets of men,
the chippers of empathy fill their hearts

enough to survive the dark and the dark.
The dungeon dwellers live quartz the size
of the grave they polish and leave behind, a fossil
that ought to collapse museums of natural history.

Romancing Lust

"The point is simply this: how tender can we bear to be? What good manners can we show as we welcome ourselves and others into our hearts?"

Rebecca Wells
Divine Secrets of the Ya-Ya Sisterhood

Mass Consumption

The summer's heat lamp swings hips
along the ocean where pubescence consumes
super-sized boys and seasoned girls
and laps the beaches of adulthood.

Discovering a male hunger, I pulled up
to the drive through window and received
my resuscitated burger and sleeve
of shoestring fries while a handful

of coeds scooped their ice cream
from a tub. The sea gulls diving
through the parking lot survive
on a boardwalk mis-shapened, lame.

THE COMPLEMENTS OF THE HOUSE

Attempting to fill its silos with French kisses,
the tongue and groove couple finishes a home
by filling a four-legged animal costume.
Engaged hardwood floors, married

straight-back chairs, sexually active
kitchen cabinets snap into place: living room,
dining room, over and under countertops.
A chimera grows corn, kids, old, but leaves

the love chain fallow. Compasses
for discoveries by unidentifiable hands
and the steel lock rust in worlds
without innovation, compassion.

Frozen in the arctic of the day
that they met, each hole mate drags
a body upon its death. The cul-de-sac
rejects the compromise but leaves behind

borders to the tongue-in-cheek puzzle.

The Ways She Moves

Once the karat and stiff
held houses together. The miner intruders
or the minor abuses braced the walls
that fixed the roofs – dependent
on the movements by women.
Before the glitter patina settled
on the living room set and bric-a-brac,
a stick or groin rib bedded the whole home matter
bruised or broken. The pioneer
in civilized control calmed
emotional, empty lives with a gem
and gym, lapis and lapdog, jade and maid.
The manipulated yoga expert
hangs by one arm
from the neck in a vintage wine bottle.
Some former classmates avoided
the domesticated animal dichotomy.
Many wild Will Hiplots labor career ceilings,
or toil at small potatoes for peanuts
without doler and dupe,
baby carriage and slick shift,
caviar and garden prick: the untempted
that leave nothing unattempted.

THE GUISE

Sitting with their feet up on
kitchen tables, women spit
emotions into little jars that
are taken for slaps on the back.

The genesis of women's words
scurries from under their chairs
across the floor through the crack
in the door. Any children that may

have fallen out of them hang
stuffed on their arms at stores,
Gucci, and teeth of the flies in
their pants were fashioned from

solid testosterone. Mary Jane,
sling-back, pumps, stiletto heels,
yet men enter and exit houses:
Everyone gets boots out of it.

BOXES OF LUST

Leapt into by mating animals,
the boxes of lust delineate
the streets as wooden cages
taming slugs or pacing beasts

using family brands of compassion.
The unique sets of keys
each of us owns to a destiny's ark
were dreamed and deeded fruitless

and placed in an atheist's drawers
in favor of chocolate coated wolves
and brief erotic teases in exchange
for security. Parents would serve loins

best by merging their children
through property rather than hiding
a son's claws in a bouquet or placing
cleavage on a store shelf for men

to wear as mustaches. If the lions
don't lie belching lamb, the most
the neighborhoods could offer other
crated cowers and roaming singles

is a variety of private kindness
grudged against city and town
and random dead end passion
sired in the back seats of cars.

Fit Response

Darwin's groins erect
wooden boxes to nurture
regret's pitter patter for eighteen years.
Hearts and minds coagulate

in taxidermists' pails,
while the libido drives
the sex emulation class
of chemists, hypnotists,

and mechanics – next stop,
via the Screen Actors' Guild,
nouveau riche.
After a century to mull behavior,

Adonis continues the Watusi,
dominating paperback erotics
and Freudian Helix; a researcher
of mating habits wades

into a computer screen, divorced
and poised. The dermatologist is
tickled by the lack of guts in monkeys
and massages the latest features.

Mutants applying the eyes' salve
practice breathing alone
in separate states.
Waiting just kills them.

Natural Disasters

Neighbors transport the occupants
of their love stretcher to the old world
of role fever where the tops and bottoms
of mating animals imitate mountains

and doctors to legitimate their parts.
Emerging from a motel room
and aping a seed's creative process,
the two practitioners of giving look

for no shelter in the lives of actors
or in heat. The cold-weathered
mattress sharers improvise each
morning's love of events while

soap operas blare from houses
that have tripped the momentum
of children pretending to be horses
that charge romance's empty plains.

TESTICLE RECEPTACLES

Sperm banks lurk with lamplight on every city corner.
In fact, the storefront oppression running along blocks
or simply overwhelming the sidewalk smiles
at the creased skirts. The scissor sisters dream
mermaids but cut curves, and trim tights avoid
loans and throw mannequins at phallic facades.
The vaults directing rivers gush shallow I love yous.
The bed and table hold a garden hose and a cup of DNA:
Bloom bloom the vase reports to ears soaking in porn,
to noses suffering osmosis, to fingers reciting pistils.
Waking Barbie palls founder along testosterone miles
through swimsuit competitions to kitchen sinks
where saturation impregnates fish eyes.
Guppies and tadpoles loot grottos, ravish bird nests.
Noah reigns the continents with grandma still kicking:
god love her. The scrotum levies burst
at the first site where weakness produces futile silt
for the no growth pearls. Loans and liens load
good edifice for disaster masters
carving initial interest into female sighs. Pears dropped
their breasts in sadness. One dog paddle
looks similar to the next. It would be vice
to live beneath a diaphragm or outside
condom bubbles that the meteorologist floats
past the haggard crowd at market. Sweet schemes
in girlhood shrouds under six feet gathering
to cat call streams across teleprompters,
and a river babbles something
about a ready vile, a wave.

LABORS OF LOVE

Neighborhood immortality,
parked in the groins of split-level
and duplex pubescence,
celebrates its own natal monuments.

Block parties and field trip
processions honor the cul-de-sacs
married to desperation and bill-fold:
A toast and traffic jam.

Poetry's generations of playmates
splash in their office schedules
and build breaths by syncopating routines
and drawing from hats commuter faces,

promising changes to old trophies and births
to the parents of their own worlds.
The mothers of perpetual labors point out
to the literal copulations elbows and knees.

Petty Thieves

With their hands groping and grabbing,
the revelers, lurking in the dark alleys
of love for a party carrying hints of money
market and stock fund, lust for each

other's wallets. The cowhide vulva
and oxblood foreskin survive the sex
by the skin of the wedding witness,
but the couple loses its grip, the muggers

having licked and sucked pocket change
while the giving of concern when life
is slipping away lies a corpse in a vault.
The pickpocket dance, a tangle of tango,

disperses boas and spats along romance
that streets were paved to embrace.

Gender Universes

After his love song and his ballet
performance, she sat upon a pile
of splinters and random baseball
bat. Tears teetered on her cheeks.

The testosterone projects break
her house's heart. He cannot touch
her world with a reach of a finger.
Eventually, he throws his hands up

and turns on the television, accepting
its engagement seduction. She
is never far away though with glue
and bows holding whole rooms

together. An assigned universe of feeling
circles the universe of action, neither
with a translator for the occasional
meeting, leaving his fault lines.

Ravishing

Alarmed and kidnapped, a tall, dark, and handsome morn-
ing gawks, entranced by the young naked woman splashing
and spraying waters and flowers among porcelains. She turned
the day on to her with brushes, and blushes and shadows and
her. Stepping out from among tubs and sinks and soaps to the
room of curtains and dress, her glistening body's heat and the
air joined forces to dry her.

With her wardrobe hanging pressed in recesses or folded in
bureau she snatches the black panties from their drawer and
with each foot arched like dolphin entering water, plunged
them into the French cuts. Pulling the lace of satin mesh until
the bikini caressed the muff of her vulva and Lycra bottom held
her cheeks as though it were two hands, she then let the elastic
waist band snap against her flesh she wore stretched over her
hips. Odysseus' Circe of the work day snapped up the loops of
a matching brassiere, threaded her arms, and caught the two
pad-less B-cups beneath her breasts and with arms akimbo
behind her back wrestled with herself using elastic material and
hooks and eyes in a game of expectation. When arms fell to
her side satisfied and the peaks of perky bosoms threatened to
pierce the thin shields of satin, she turned sideways and with
a sigh looked at herself in the wall's reflecting pool. From the
closet in fever, the impassioned pursuer of suits slipped into a
silk blouse and pushed each bone nipple through its slit, top to
bottom and with her own hands caressed the worm's work that
gave up at the kisses of hidden flesh that pecked and dropped
creases to her waist. Her giving body to the color of her short-
sleeved bodice demanded the colored pattern of the skirt. The
Joan of abs stepped into the fray of linings, seams, hems and
pulled to meet, mate, and overlap her top at the tight pannier's

waist. Again, akimbo she pinned herself over hook, eye, and zipper until she had her way with them. A park's lunchtime tan was all the nylon hosiery or sheer netting her legs needed today to flash their dominion over men. At the bottom of the tiny room of her hangers that hold ghost of her past and future, her high heels stood ready to stand between her confident feet and the hard day ahead. One by one she kicked them on. A last look in the now magic mirror revealed the cutlass curves of desire. She strode to the door fresh but sassy.

After the nuisance elbows and groping of public transportation, the dominatrix entered the long erected building. She rose to the upper floors. From the first step into the punch clock coliseum to the last stride of the workday from her control center she sacked. The *Have a good day* of the many male sirens tore at their own clothes and molested their daydreams in men's rooms, cold bare apartments.

Voyeur

From behind the bushes outside
the windows, I expose incredible
couples with my camera and excite
myself with irony: The lovers have

no love. My pornography has arrested
enough marriages and mates to occupy
a thousand brothels. Sleepwalking affairs
perform in my lens. First, the larger humps

of muscle possess and girls take note
and weigh themselves. Then, men
and women fall in love with their minor
economies and haggle over appearance

and favors. I pan from coast to coast
and bedrooms frame acts of the American
Dream in abandon: museum furniture
marketed for its rights of reproduction.

Wow Vow

HAL

" . . . I don't want to get too personal, but do you have a
good relationship with your wife? Are you close with her?"

Callie Khouri
Thelma and Louise

Wow Vow

Marriage bottles behavior and delivers it
to the neighborhoods or pumps it
from reservoirs through pipes
into homes where children bathe,

teens wash cars, and parents drink
a quart a day. No family survives
without the refreshing rituals
that seem to fall from the sky

and run down our streets. A wedding
and front lawn give birth to a civil nation,
and all is emptied from the world ever after.
Unquenched by commitment's cupped hands,

the quirk lovers improvise their promises
over and around the rocks of the forest.

BIOLOGICAL DISTRACTION

Husbands and wives fill houses
with doodads and two strangers.
Heavy appliances dangle at the ends
of cords for dinner guests and plug

holes in the kitchens and basements.
Boys and girls take up nooks in rooms
as reports to the tax man that novelty
creatures can join at the groin.

Home entertainment centers clog
the hallways and drains with gluttony.
Should the houses burst, belt ways
are loosened and driveways shifted.

When the corner decorations run
away with strangers of their own to fill
houses for themselves, the old shoppers
who recognize mirrors, throw them out.

THE WEBSTERS ET AL

Father's fetishes, mother's moods,
an aunt's angst, are wrapped in love
to celebrate with friends and spouses
who also have families. The private

parties attempt to exchange the same
dictionaries but spellbind each other
with intimacies' drills: attitude's
confetti and a foreign tongue.

After the misspelled holidays and holes
in the walls, the invisible line divides
the wine and roses. The personal
libraries are covered in the dust

of shopping malls and sporting events.
The gulf of the two work weeks
gulps hard on Saturday and Sunday:
gondola and golf. A home finds itself

no room in the excavated faces
or in book-marked voices, and a home
finds itself no room in the shelved
voices or in archived faces. When

a gift excites outside the silk
and lace of memory's lexicon,
the differences between abridge their
season into the bones of the crafters.

Sports Trivia

When the trophies jump from the mantel
or knock over their glass cases,
the mothers and fathers are roused
from their positions along the champion

assembly line to put the trash out to the curb.
With the game of parenting model children
in shards, the remote losers outfit stadiums
with professional football teams

and their wives make concessions by hand.
The sore sports use their couched backs
to defend against accusations of children
lugging barrels of body parts through

the streets and onto adulthood's front lawns.
The next generation's parade of contenders
enter matrimony's rings to cast
figurines of short-lived, world-class hope.

CHEMICAL WASTE

A sibling's nape, echoes of an uncle's phony laugh,
the scent of mother's soap, and we begin our
experiment by calling ourselves chemists. While
fermenting explosive amounts of cosmetics and

muscle enhancers, we then grind human genitalia
into children who lament parents, strangers to each
other, who laminate with gasoline and kitchen
cleaning products a family. There is pop,

and here's to the bystanders bandaged in chocolate
and petals! The beakers shattered in the fireplace;
a wrinkle sweeps across lab coats: The house
cannot but grow as cold as law degrees.

Addicted to memory and fearful of balms
posing as acids, we swish old wishes and splash
our past, bathers, fixing our flesh for pharmacy,
baking soda to love's bone dust alchemy.

SLUT

Even though she gives birth
to addiction and pushes dogs
from her breasts, she is brave:
The mirror for women undressed,

a teacher for the unseen, should
there be a student anywhere.
All her pleasure has been given up
for the jackpot of bills and loose coin

bilked from money machines
with removable pants who travel
from bed to bed. She spreads her legs
to yawn and never wants to wake up.

During her first cry she swallowed
her diamond lodging it in her heart,
neither mined by her or anyone else.
Her stand on a corner is myth.

She too plays violin for young men
who lay the streets they piss on
drunk from images that fathers
and mothers poured into their eyes.

But she stretches her own gut.

No Match

"Most people marry other people's mates."

Maya Angelou

Most people marry other people's mates.

Gain's forced romance
and faith's long lonely life
compose the ready-or-not and confused
cry-babies in shopping malls.

The pressure between old fashioned fun
and the birth canal no longer bring one
and one to the altar, and yet the generational Ark
must be pregnant with mothers and fathers.

Aristophanes' Yin and Yang may yet
bump into each other in a bed though.

Or there may be no crew: a drifting dingy
and Ishmael and Edna thrashing in the water.

Brave Heart

Random couplings stay stupid to the crutches
kicked out from under each bundle of nerves.
Family plans leave outside the houses
the body's long crumple to the cemetery:
a barking back weighs on handicapped muscles
where heart disease and kidney failure mix
their potion. A grey wave disorients wild
imaginations from a second body present.
Caught by surprise with spouses,
marriages celebrating numbers end
plotting separate ways with bitter pills,
each stranger using a magnifying glass
on the other. The distractions of babies
and chores mesmerize occupants
of another planet. The loner through
it all embraces the degeneration of the body
and mind, an affair toward opening eyes.

Marriage in Wonderland

Often a house where a couple of cowards
pretend to hide from cities that lick their chops
just outside the door and where mice wave
good-bye to friends from windows, marriage

lies folded in drawers until two consenting adults
wear theirs as shirts, so that arms and legs are free
to create by giving each day, and so they may be
removed for achieving what only sex can clean.

Fabrication

Though bath and front stairs thread contrary,
law suits and business suits
weave lingerie and boxer shorts.
Futile needle eyes aim to wink at shrinks.
The intimate yarn about a naked public
lays about mammary glands
that wean muscular upper bodies to fatty hips.
Delusion may insist otherwise,
but Fanny sits around a bedroom
waiting for some emperor.
Uniformed officers in pants
take Domestica by norm.
Phones, loudspeakers,
and email accounts suck carnal knowledge
and compassion from mingling breaths.
The news bulletin announces
the proclamation that for fun
find a stadium or parking lot.
The cook drums fingers on her pots until
as spoon slips apple sauce past wrinkles.
Tailgate parties prefer the cemetery
to chicken soup.

LIVE AT THE ZONE

A head and lyre, buried on
the island of Lesbos, accompany
each other to the surface of paper,
clefs of orgasmic complaints.

Archeologists shoveling with pens,
unearth hetero and homo flecks
for worlds to examine and discover
themselves: The calm waters crack.

A swan's feather dusts and tickles
each epoch to test for humanity.
Everybody's favorite poems
have always looked over their

shoulders to bring Apollo to passion.
Fingers press the frown's furrows
into chords and the rocks and trees
sprout feet: any age sex inspires.

Valentine Party

Romantic couples have long hung
their faces on coat hooks at the end
of love. Cupid's Hell Game
adds heads to its wall, pusses of

Guy and Flighty stiff with kisses
gone bitter. Many pairs of lips
save face to lust another day
but even Blue Beard's bore's mask

will decorate the hall. Each nursing
home passed by passionate pimples
stores orgasm's moping cheeks
mopping floors from wheelchairs.

Just outside, the herds and fleas
sing "sip life's greatest refreshment
while you may, and then my friend
celebrate alone until you decay."

Pop

The storybook's pages popped out
into the rooms of the house where she
now lives. Every house on her street
was constructed in the same manner.

Small cities outside the neighborhood
sprang from Dante's Inferno. In the state
capital pinstriped men pass judgment:
Barbie dolls hanged from arms of husbands –

single mothers to the pitch of poverty.
To the west clitori are manicured
with seashells; to the east head strong
women bathe in acid. From the nightmares

waiting for dimension in the light of yet
another day, no children startle with hope
when authors become despots and fix
their pens around their subjects.

Family Fun

Margaret

"Well, I!---just remarked that!—one of th' no-neck monsters messed up m' lovely lace dress so I got t'---cha-a-ange. . . ."

Tennessee Williams
Cat On a Hot Tin Roof

FOLK ART

Into the empty grandstand seats,
the synchronized living competition
splashes its families' accroutrements
and legal papers. The stacks

of towels sandbag attempts at all
other sports by choking children
spotting the water's edge. Right arms
raised signal positions in the pool

that spell out some reason for breathing.
Lifted left arms inform commuters
of turns. The vortex to coordination
dizzies awkward treaders dotting

the business districts with bathing caps
while it sucks at funeral parlors in cities
and suburbs. The losers walk boards
and planks gargling soup kitchen therapy

and submerge, while the ballet bathers
hold their noses on queues. Getting
their kicks from the Champaign of stocks
and nepotistic bonds, the team strokes

the American dream with house paint
and rescues cramped quarters with life
insurance. Eccentric humans, waist deep
in cooperation, squat with mediocrity,

dive with fellow divers, and spritz

with mellow spritzers. Every year
champion communities dry by design
in retirement where they bow in tandem.

LULLABY

Suzie Q. puffs a pillow, pulls a false
consciousness to her chin, and opens
her eyes. Masculine roots, prefixes,
and suffixes twist a dilated tongue

into a dream world of apology and
declension. Ballet slippers mold feet
and measure steps in a morning
of abandoned tires, random fences,

and logs across rivers to kitchens
and kids. The marriages hatched
from shotgun shells sizzle sunny
soul mates up. How does an egg

within an egg wring a new species
from a little girl's hands? Woven
of grunts and grinds the security
blanket subjugates emotions, period

Birth Day Party

Miscarried motherhood gave birth
to a woman. The reward
for labor walks without first a crawl,
a prize beneath which men cry.
Misfortune in miss, ms buried itself
under soiled boxer shorts
and sprouted valued kisses.
The infant bears a foreign tongue
on its taste for emotion.
The city streets wag to tonsils
articulating a planet saved
from nature and politics.
Oh, suspends a ball, a globe on an edge
much needed for the new kind and love.

GRETEL TO NAIVE

From ladle to grave her mother's apron
blindfolded her while the Hansel young boy
in his father's voice reassured
the peek-a-boo heroine of her
good fortune by telling horror stories
of what she was missing.
The parental faces parse par's parcel
for the comfort of community.
Buried beneath the foundations
of other people's houses, the intimacy
once possible for each cookie cutter character
never blossoms. Protest drives
up and down the avenue in a backhoe
merely excavate the expressway
to apartments waiting for bitterness
on different sides of town. On this late date,
the manicured front lawn tickles toes.

Terrorized

Terrorists strap sport utility vehicles
to their bodies and from themselves
mask with oceans their suburban
self-absorption and the women

lugging water to shacks of hungry
children. When the guerillas escape
on highways that lead to vacation
homes, ancient city squares squat into

the squalor wreckage of weathered huts.
The long drive by faceless murderers
into the enemy territory to abandon
starvation bombs strips survivors

of all convention. Bones of farmers
and clerks emerge the white picket
fences that real estate agents, training
recruits in the acts of avarice, declare

uninfested. The will of the peasant
becomes a refugee and roams
the countryside for a beggar's plan.
Pastoral herds captured by tourists

with cameras have two-legged
steers and feed the sons of fat
fathers coaching football teams.

Totalitarian Jig Gig

When dancing with the jailor,
innocence doesn't jingle
and the partners syncopate the finale
to the choreography.
A cell also gets in the way
of the rhythm, and the music's key
frees the inmate from thought outdoors.
The convict's movements collaborate
with a court's chug and thug.
Sitting on the bunk
points out the bunk until the guard
jiggles another wallflower using a spoon
to tunnel from the mess.
Unlocking the prison gate
behind the eyes opens Zen's cliché wilderness,
but even the guilty bank robber
may lose himself in the forest.
A far away meadow that possesses options
for revenge relaxes the ribcage in the evening.
Exiles jitterbug with tailors
according to tyranny's tango
witness who also sings bars and stripes forever.
The other shoe flops with a charge
and limp limbs. Skipping the protest
the worker, who never spends
his jumping jack cash,
plays the clown to a crown.

PHILOMELA'S READING

Nightingales form flocks for comfort
whenever they are more than one.
When alone, they perch themselves
at the ends of telephone wire.

Men cannot understand the behavior
or speech of the thrice caged creatures.
But the daily coronations of broad
shoulders and narrow hips that gave

birth to the story of the hunt put
the world to sleep and escaped blame.
Stripped of power, species, and song,
the flesh in feathers, tell their tales

in poems as opaque as tar, only now
being unlocked by mutants
with combination numbers. The convict
without bars doesn't understand

until her body sings through his.

ISLE OF MAN

The rocks sing and sailors die,
so men furnish dwellings with diamonds
to placate disaster and return
to the open intimacies of sports.

Along the masts and bows of club houses
and bar rooms the athletes fill their ears
with bees' wax while gambling on
the hometown team. Vasco da Gama

and Admiral Perry embrace each other
through parking lots when the expedition
has stumbled upon harbor time
where the dangerous maneuvers begin.

Through a sea sick periscope, Babe Ruth
is plucked from on deck by Scylla's cliff,
a golfing buddy loses to Charybdis'
porcelain hole in one, while the ship's

boulders and ledges tour their own emotions
that wade from the coastline to greet them.
Counting the syllables to their first songs,
women have not set foot on this island.

CHAERONEA'S CONQUERORS

> "They were in two layers, packed like sardines. You could
> still see where the Macedonian lances smashed arms, ribs,
> skulls . . . Most extraordinary thing I've ever seen."

Tom Stoppard

The sacred band of husbands
and their meatloaves shield themselves
against the glare of lovers who live
beyond biology's trick and muscle's wealth.

As children, the hoplites for progeny
are put to sleep beneath sheets of brass
and become outrageous fortune
enslaving the smaller bones allowed to move.

Rattled bedrooms and scrambled eggs
bring patriarchal landscapes to the senses
of pubescent daughters who dreamed
of fields as open as their eyes.

Girlfriends of officers-in-training learn
the threatening terrain, with slow acceptance:
farm tools, city buildings and the blue
strobes of police cars until breathing within

the bachelor herd is of suburban air
to accomplices meeting each other
to commiserate around the overlooked baubles
of bodies left to be picked at and guarded.

Womb warriors in wedding bands defend
themselves against the barbaric bunkers
of their own sexuality marshaling rice
and babies and armed mothers sold.

Love Story

In a bedroom, a wallet unfolds and a purse
opens to the game of hide and silk. When
young, a bolt dreamed someone else's
career plan and a bull used office furniture

to masturbate, olé. From opposite suburban
towns the two tongs of a money clip
traveled meeting as luck couldn't avoid
in the financial district around a cashed

pay check. The smooth finger and calloused
thumb work their magnetism into pockets
of least resistance and then lie back
holding cigarettes. Eventually pregnant

as a house, the Wells Fargo money sack
gushes a home's unlimited accessories,
the lust for oil wells giving birth
to Cornucopias' orgasms along the streets.

Family Business

Family business begins with clergy
cashing checks by investors after
they all have read someone's fortune
in a diamond. A man and a woman

hit the wresting mats on an island
landscaped for the purpose where
cupid's bankruptcy is admitted
into their ledger: Whoever gets pinned

gets pregnant. Mom and pop enter
the picture where the deals have
been made. As the product line ages
and ferments enough to be sold

or given away, the shares are divested
though looting occurs slowly.
Siblings pluck the hairs from
the heads of the bosses. Neighbors

only notice the mirror in the store
window, so the police are never called.
By the time owners are boarded up, good
buyers fall in love with family business.

X-Rated

In the boudoir of two colors the easy
reading of children fills tool boxes
with rattles and thumbs. Love
can't be shaken from blunt tongues

insisting for fifty years with groin
and groan. Race relations concern
the residents of the North and South
Poles in a dream of schoolyard games

among us and them. Each evening
married couples masturbate in each
others arms, while watching actors
with diamonds and knees. Adult

movies hold the high school gym
class hostage until social security
checks arrive. Sex's prism never
enlightens the activities wrinkling

sheets and pillows, nor does happily
ever after catch the sun into ribbons
across the sky. But then these are
today's pigments that stain giving.

THE WOMAN WRESTLER

She uses her body to steal
men's wallets. She'd tell a judge that she
performs a kind of CPR

and collects a fee for the service.
A childhood pout drew boys
from whom to choose and later curves
caused testosterone that then lost

control of the age of wheels.
Her presence became the tool
that almost evened the score she had
with uncles, brother, father. In marriages

men are men and busier than golf,
and tennis is the intimacy of women.
She becomes a wrinkled vault with gold
and jewels oozing out from around

its door, and any man who isn't enraged
at himself and vacationing with an intern,
remains a boy showing off to his dad.

Body Language

"Stroke your body's contours. Do you like what you feel?
Try saying something appreciative to each part of your-
self. It may be difficult at first."

Wendy Sanford
The New Our Bodies, Ourselves

Jingle on the Boardwalk

Americans want their poetry to kiss
them on the mouth in public
and hang on them through their day
or forget it. So bus loads

of rhyme schemers throw themselves
at pedestrians at every stop.
The attention drives bystanders
and fawners to cheap hotels

where the Homer kings memorize
the spray of words around ballparks.
When a week at "top ten" shakes
a pant leg free of humming,

the fans strike out to revise the play,
and the Coca-Cola crowd
turns on the pouts for the new gush
from pucker prosody rushing

to their sides. There is never mind
for the choirs lodged in bookcases.
Even though engaged at rendezvous
behind closed curtains, intuition

and language perform the orgasms
of several lifetimes. Should magnets
working their magic on prefab
nostalgia generate the pursuits

of intimacy, a subtle song travels

from ancient feet through hearts
to first breath in the world.

Blueprint

The only two postures of women,
facilitator or bitch, saw and hammer
for men's desires. The rainy days
together are measured, cut, and nailed

behind lipstick on an ark ramming
sunset. All species bear down when
replying to tomorrow's letters.
But the print left by the captain

and crew, punching out the eye
of god with a hull, reads as though
there are only two narrow alley ways
when the meadows greet us all.

Good marrow to the tool box,
a good wind, and raw materials
tickling the penis. The prop
with the amended dictionary on

its head opens to a fan's rainbow: tree,
upward facing dog: ashtanga. If only
the carpenters could negotiate the horizon,
party planners might stop the barking.

Boy Meets Girl

His vanity requires no response
and breaks a woman's mirror:
One woman, hardly aware
of her departed lover, slips

into her make up, whereupon
a second accepts the acting life.
For Hollywood off Broadway,
she donates body parts to the poverty

of a man's senses of self. A great
nothing blows her skirt up, and she
embeds her feet into the cement
of her shadow. With his boar's head

pelvis and oyster in hand like his neighbor,
Mr. Fillmore buries himself in toys
leaving behind a pile of Mimi scouring
the shallow years for a woman.

Casanova's Bossa Nova

The dance shoes, seduction
and coercion, owned by male feet,
roam floors that beg for chandeliers.
In search of flat-footed beauty

and a bed, where ever they might be,
the handsome conversation attracts
female followers trading on the smiles
of curves. Dizzying, the next steps

leave dresses dipped and hung over
with a purse and heart opened at
their tops. The wallflowers can't say
when the tango with the rag doll began,

but witnesses toasted a conga line
of would-be brides that transcend
a retirement community in Florida,
each giving up her precious moments

on Earth to fandango's flimflam.

Don Juan in America

Women in foamy tubs love him
touched up and glossy.
His two-dimensional eyes seem
to embrace the spiritual needs

moving the lips of women to speak
in tongues. When the bubbles lie
tepid, the day can be greeted
with the remaining enthusiasm.

If his blue ink dots bulged
into life and into the champagne
of emotion, it would not be
with empathy but the way

a conquistador spotted easy real
estate through a tube. Should
he ever grace the dynamism
of a woman's bare arms, he would

shrink to the shoot of a new issue
by way of fear or disgust. The blest
would dry herself and own
the smell of resin on her breasts.

ROMEO'S RUSE

As evenings grow to masks
and violence, families can
pull girls from dance floors
and from their bedroom windows

but Romeo leaves his knife
around and promises of wealth.
As though loving were an accident
of competition, the romantic boys

drag behind them bodies that
the churches sort for marriage
and tombs. Those who survive
as men hold corpses in their chests.

The women who breathe drown
in elixirs. Juliette's wiser bedtime
stories, antidote to a boy's dreams,
never dispense into a daughter's ear.

Flora

The agency in the colony opens
its exotic petals each morning
in fertilized homeland. Eyes stretch
a map as far as they and sea.
Snagged peninsulas sag to sharpen
a point for possible escape
though the sensual fish nets harness
a lust to please deep into farm country.
An ocean marinades and pickles
to inject a collusion cargo,
domestic animals, and a hint
of wild goose. When the paddies
and bogs produce mock ceremonies
with a smile, when legs sing without string,
longitude and latitude disappear.
Raw materials relax into the flow of things.
Arms put down and all embrace,
if ever loaded onto the trunk.
With inner resource, the island
reinforces the charts and oral description;
accommodation lacks hip movements.
Even sand spits enjoy their lot.
Evolutionary biology suggests
organs may not have survived
for original desires. However,
the flowering remains suspect.

THE TITANIC SEA

"their cries rising in waves"

William Carlos Williams

Women and children, flailing
rags in the wind, rescue lifeboats
sardined with First World families
snubbing each other for fun. The same
bold dories sailing the silent backs
for which soccer dads expect their wives
to produce salt water. Beggars don't dream
the provider to drive a bargain
in a minivan and come home
with a new pool to exploit.
The tears during sales drown out
the distant mooring moaning
and seething according to moon moods.
The win passes through cheesecloth poverty.
Besides starboard and crooks,
if not the spines bending for pennies,
then the chubby family watching television.

No thank you, says the innocent jellyfish
demanding new Nikes for himself
all over the world while busy
burning foreign oil around the town.
First mate, do something to rock
craft enough to keep it from flipping over,
flares from the eyes in kitchens across the land.

The keel grooves upon the heads

and between the neck and shoulders
that mark the caste at whom tourists wave
traumatize generations streaming
along the streets in filthy cities.
No person would want to trade a pillow
for a ledge, even for two nights on Everest.
So if the drifting culture can't make headway
through the currency current to dryness,
the emergency teams improvise
to maintain their grip on their gunwales.
The buoyant safari for some rich soil
would set down the capitalist survivors
anywhere they swished in pitch toil,
but the vacation crew paddles behinds.

DOWNTOWN

Taxicabs carrying the coat hangers idle,
waiting outside while the men in houses
of congress map ways for women to seek
the back seats. To double back at this point

into the journey endangers schoolchildren
learning respect for whom they are not.
While legislating a boulevard to the birth
of a city, the heartland stands between

the two legs of a story with mask on
and palms open at the threshold of freedom
and justice, the twins crying for their day.
The placards read, "Pay the fare and send

the hackney home," a compass for frightened
men in the wilderness of conscious love.
Citizens traveling together, avoiding alleys
of a mob's mind, each wear shoes

that are right for each of them. Tipping
the balance of momentum from yesterday,
shoulders bent on power can't come
to terms: maimed with twenty years to life.

ATTENTION

She lives alone in a corner of his eye.
He owns the land before her
like a rock that becomes an apple.
Temptation and the hard place of poverty

drives her to project that her knowledge
of his surface means possession.
The mass of his lifelessness out weighs
the gilt glinting on his jagged shadows.

His rubbing of his lidded cornea flushes
the obstruction from his panorama,
and she moves to find another home
in the periphery of her life.

ACCESSORIES

"Where woman have been a luxury for man . . ."

Adrienne Rich

Having purchased luxury for the passenger seats
of their life journeys, the young drivers
speed off as though warrantees came
with the navigator of nothing.
On the crowded highway boredom's sun
and rain glancing off the precious goods
requires the sweep and visors of distraction.
Raking money into the backyards,
arranging toys at the peripheries
of property, at first the fun seems real.
Then, the many dollars tickling cause calluses
until vaults crush the vital V-8s
of subtle perception and agony
expresses itself by infliction.
Of course the poor and defenseless masses
pay first and a great price, but then
possessions go through re-evaluation
of their financial and accommodating worth.
The leather upholstery now carries
wrinkled cow hide satchels emptied
of their prestige and giggles. Either
another gift to blunted sensibilities comes
along for the ride and Cubic-Z's long face
to the adventurer's grave
stays at home steaming curtains
or the excessorized safari loses its caddy.

Her Morning Gargle

Pickled in an intimate language
and encumbered in a pool
formed by stage lighting
without the cool cucumber fins,
whispers, amplified, stay within their lines.
Big girls feign death in a voice box
and douse themselves in vinegar
in the hops that someone nails it shut.
Before saturation boys don't stand
a chance. Cores with motored mouths
order breakfast, battlefields, and all
the gears to line up for a smile.
If wrestling words pinned leading men,
the ten-year-old rat nest would have
Sir Lawrence Olivier dissected
and still under a glass case.

Sponges in their wild habitat
study salt and spit back some
other body's deep thoughts.
Crisp energy drowns one thread
at a time until silk raises its flag.
The short story draws out a flowing curtain.
The petite echo chambers
protect with a distant father air.
The fight for a genuine larynx
settles sediment in the barrel bottom
where angling jaws place their hands
as though they own it.

Magic by Design

Over mammary glands and hips,
the flesh chador dissolves the person
peering through the coiffure.
The old secret formula brand new.
A veil of skin melts the particular
and potential from the good senses of men.
Testosterone city saves the sin of knowing
for carnal examinations. Curves'
pores, texture, and fashion
stitch size to its power,
and a father gives away a fetish.
Dog owners and cowboys
understand their animals.
Dermatological hijabs bear
responsibility for exposing anything
other than sweetheart and bitch,
robe the spectrum in a baby-talk
shadow. Stoned into a squawk
the vanishing character beneath
nape and legs surrenders it scarf
to the release of brawn.
In order to remain a virgin to awakening
the burqa broad vaporizes the psyche
guilty of embracing its dream.
And so a frontier's man again moralizes
drinking water's reflection into tribes.

BODY LANGUAGE

Once a woman vacates her place,
post-traumatic stress invades
her nervous system and the malls
and stadiums need interpreters to stand.

The slow rapes of the free wills
and personalities of millennia's
daughters reverberate a gender
for generations. On their cues

kitchen carcasses in doilies stay put,
and in men's voices talk louder –
but crane their necks to watch
the constructions of new language.

I'd love to wrap my tongue around
one of those unformed words,
but I pull up in my sport car
an hundred years too early

of the date. I still don't have
a name for the demonstration
that causes me to dance a poem.

Books Available from Gival Press
Poetry

Adamah: Poème by Céline Zins; translation by Peter Schulman
    ISBN 13: 978-1-928589-46-4, $15.00
    This bilingual (French/English) collection by an eminent French poet/
    writer is adeptly translated in this premiere edition.

Bones Washed With Wine: Flint Shards from Sussex and Bliss
by Jeff Mann
    ISBN 13: 978-1-928589-14-3, $15.00
    Includes the 1999 Gival Press Poetry Award winning collection. Jeff
    Mann is "a poet to treasure both for the wealth of his language and the
    generosity of his spirit."
    — Edward Falco, author of *Acid*

Canciones para sola cuerda / Songs for a Single String
by Jesús Gardea; English translation by Robert L. Giron
    ISBN 13: 978-1-928589-09-9, $15.00
    Finalist for the 2003 Violet Crown Book Award—Literary Prose &
    Poetry. Love poems, with echoes of Neruda à la Mexicana, Gardea
    writes about the primeval quest for the perfect woman.

Dervish by Gerard Wozek
    ISBN 13: 978-1-928589-11-2, $15.00
    Winner of the 2000 Gival Press Poetry Award / Finalist for the 2002
    Violet Crown Book Award—Literary Prose & Poetry.
    "By jove, these poems shimmer."
    —Gerry Gomez Pearlberg, author of *Mr. Bluebird*

The Great Canopy by Paula Goldman
    ISBN 13: 1-928589-31-0, $15.00
    Winner of the 2004 Gival Press Poetry Award / 2006 Independent
    Publisher Book Award—Honorable Mention for Poetry
    "Under this canopy we experience the physicality of the body through
    Goldman's wonderfully muscular verse as well the analytics of a mind
    that tackles the meaning of Orpheus or the notion of desire."
    — Richard Jackson, author of *Half Lives*

Honey by Richard Carr
ISBN 13: 978-1-928589-45-7, $15.00
Winner of the Gival Press Poetry Award
"*Honey* is a tour de force. Comprised of 100 electrifying microsonnets .
. . The whole sequence creates a narrative that becomes, like the Hapax
Legomenon, a form that occurs only once in a literature."
—Barbara Louise Ungar, author of *The Origin of the Milky Way*

Let Orpheus Take Your Hand by George Klawitter
ISBN 13: 978-1-928589-16-7, $15.00
Winner of the 2001 Gival Press Poetry Award
A thought provoking work that mixes the spiritual with stealthy desire,
with Orpheus leading us out of the pit.

Metamorphosis of the Serpent God by Robert L. Giron
ISBN 13: 978-1-928589-07-5, $12.00
This collection "...embraces the past and the present, ethnic and sexual
identity, themes both mythical and personal."
—*The Midwest Book Review*

Museum of False Starts by Chip Livingston
ISBN 13: 978-1-928589-49-5, $15.00
Livingston - a gay Mvskoki poet - presents a new approach to poetry
through his experience.
"...Chip Livingston makes the ordinary exotic, erotic and
extraordinary."—Ai

On the Altar of Greece by Donna J. Gelagotis Lee
ISBN 13: 978-1-92-8589-36-5, $15.00
Winner of the 2005 Gival Press Poetry Award / 2007 Eric Hoffer Book
Award: Notable for Art Category
"...*On the Altar of Greece* is like a good travel guide: it transforms reader
into visitor and nearly into resident. It takes the visitor to the authentic
places that few tourists find, places delightful yet still surprising, safe yet
unexpected...."
—by Simmons B. Buntin, editor of *Terrain.org* Blog

On the Tongue by Jeff Mann
ISBN 13: 978-1-928589-35-8, $15.00
"...These poems are ...nothing short of extraordinary."
—Trebor Healey, author of *Sweet Son of Pan*

The Nature Sonnets by Jill Williams
  ISBN 13: 978-1-928589-10-5, $8.95
  An innovative collection of sonnets that speaks to the cycle of nature and
  life, crafted with wit and clarity. "Refreshing and pleasing."
— Miles David Moore, author of *The Bears of Paris*

The Origin of the Milky Way by Barbara Louise Ungar
  ISBN 13: 978-1-928589-39-6, $15.00
  Winner of the 2006 Gival Press Poetry Award
  "...a fearless, unflinching collection about birth and motherhood, the
  transformation of bodies. Ungar's poems are honestly brutal, candidly
  tender. Their primal immediacy and intense intimacy are realized
  through her dazzling sense of craft. Ungar delivers a wonderful,
  sensuous, visceral poetry." —Denise Duhamel

Poetic Voices Without Borders edited by Robert L. Giron
  ISBN 13: 978-1-928589-30-3, $20.00
  2006 Writer's Notes Magazine Book Award—Notable for Art / 2006
  Independent Publisher Book Award—Honorable Mention for Anthology
  An international anthology of poetry in English, French, and Spanish,
  including work by Grace Cavalieri, Jewell Gomez, Joy Harjo, Peter
  Klappert, Jaime Manrique, C.M. Mayo, E. Ethelbert Miller, Richard
  Peabody, Myra Sklarew and many others.

Poetic Voices Without Borders 2, edited by Robert L. Giron
  ISBN 13: 978-1-928589-43-3, $20.00
  Honorable Mention for Poetry—2009 San Francisco Book Festival.
  Featuring poets Grace Cavalieri, Rita Dove, Dana Gioia, Joy Harjo,
  Peter Klappert, Philip Levine, Gloria Vando, and many other fine poets
  in English, French, and Spanish.

Prosody in England and Elsewhere:
A Comparative Approach by Leonardo Malcovati
  ISBN 13: 978-1-928589-26-6, $20.00
  The perfect tool for the poet but written for a non-specialist audience.

Protection by Gregg Shapiro
  ISBN 13: 978-1-928589-41-9, $15.00
  "Gregg Shapiro's stunning debut marks the arrival of a new master poet
  on the scene. His work blows me away."
  —Greg Herren, author of *Mardi Gras Mambo*